Getting To Know You

By Jeanne McSweeney and Charles Leocha

with contributions from

Diane Slezak Scholfield, Susan Vreeland, and James Thompson

World Leisure Corporation

Copyright © 1992 by World Leisure Corporation
PO Box 160, Hampstead, NH 03841

Printed in the United States by Dickinson Press, Grand Rapids, MI
Cover design: Joshua Hayes, Stormship Studios, Arlington, MA

Distributed to the trade in USA and Canada by The Talman Company,
131 Spring Street, Suite 201E-N, New York, NY 10012; tel. (212) 431-7175

Distributed to Stars & Stripes Bookstores, Mail Order and Special Sales by
World Leisure Corporation, 177 Paris Street, Boston, MA 02128
tel. (617) 569-1966, fax (617) 561-7654

ISBN: 0-915009-23-4

Introduction

This book is intended to be a catalyst
for intriguing and insightful conversations.

It really doesn't matter how much or how little
you feel you may already know someone—
you may have been married for years
and still be surprised by some of your partner's
answers to the questions you'll find here.

When we started talking about this book with friends—parents, siblings, cousins, actors, teachers, newlyweds, never-weds—they asked to join the effort and began to contribute ideas of their own.

This is a distillation of that collective wisdom based on hundreds of attempts at successful and not-so-successful relationships.

These questions have been created to bring out more than "Yes," "No," or "Maybe" answers. We hope they will lead to further discussion— "Why," "How," "What," or "Tell me more," although not spelled out, are implied.

Slowly savor this book
and the resulting conversations, laughter
and shared sense of discovery. The questions and
activities are deliberately not in any order—they are
yours to go through at random.

Getting to know another person should
most of all be a lot of fun.
We hope you discover more about yourself,
as well as one another, in the process.

Jeanne McSweeney
&
Charlie Leocha

The Authors
Charlie Leocha, an internationally renowned travel writer,
is author of *Ski Europe, Skiing America,* and *Eastern Germany.*
When not on ski slopes or airplanes, he hangs out in smoky bars.
His heroes are Zorba the Greek, Nietzsche and David Black.
His pet peeve is people calling him the "Accidental Tourist."
Jeanne McSweeney (yes, it does rhyme) is a would-be Rockette
who in real life is an advertising type and college instructor.
She lives with two cats she hopes will soon enter their tenth life.

Other contributors
Diane Slezak Scholfield is an award-winning writer who likes
random travel, soulful ballads, good conversation and her husband,
not necessarily in that order. In between summers paddling and
writing along the Canadian west coast, **Susan Vreeland** ignites the
creative spark in Southern California high school students.
James Thompson, of Old Colony Editorial Associates, finds
hidden treasures in manuscripts and flea markets.

Getting To Know You

"The meeting of two personalities
is like the contact of two chemical substances:
if there is any reaction, both are transformed."
—Carl Jung

"If a man does not make new acquaintances
as he advances through life,
he will soon find himself left alone."
—Samuel Johnson

"Questions are never indiscreet; answers sometimes are."
—Oscar Wilde

1. Who makes you laugh
   more than anyone in the world?

2. If, like the characters in The Wizard
   of Oz, you could choose
     a heart,
     courage,
     or a brain—
   which would you take?

3. *"I never forget a face, but in your case I'll make an exception."*

  —*Groucho Marx*

  Are you better at remembering names or faces?
  Do you have any tricks you use to remember names?

4. If you could spend one day with anyone in history, from the arts, politics, religion or any other field, whom would you choose?

5. Describe your best friend from childhood. What did you like most about him or her?

6. Is your current best friend anything like your best childhood friend?

7. If you could choose your own first name, what would it be?

8. Pick an interest you have that the other knows little or nothing about. Spend some time sharing and learning about it.

9. Other than your parents, what man and what woman have had the biggest effect on your life?

10. *"The best way to keep your word is not to give it."* —*Napoleon*

    Have you ever had to go back on your word? How did it make you feel?

11. If money were no object, what would you choose for your profession?

12. Narrate in detail the most vivid *good* childhood memory you have.

13. Who was your childhood idol?

14. If you could have one fabric next to your skin, what would it be?

15. Play each other's favorite board game.

16. *"When I use a word,"* Humpty Dumpty
said in a rather scornful tone, *"it means
just what I choose it to mean—
neither more nor less."*

—Lewis Carroll,
Through the Looking-Glass

Get a word-a-day calendar.
Use it together to challenge and expand
your vocabularies.

17. *"I am a great believer in luck,
and I find the harder I work
the more I have of it."*

—*Stephen Leacock*

Do you believe in luck?
What is the luckiest thing that ever
happened to you?

18. What is your all-time favorite movie?
    Rent it or go see it together.

19. Have you ever been on television?
    Do you want to be?

20. Visit each other's childhood home; if
    that's not possible, describe it in detail
    (with photos if you have them).
    Talk about the memories conjured up.

21. What was the all-time favorite job you ever had?

22. Have you ever bought a big bargain only to find out that it wasn't such a good bargain after all? How did that make you feel? Stupid, taken advantage of, indifferent?

23. Did you ever have a vacation you couldn't wait to be over?

24. To which magazines do you subscribe?
    What were they five years ago?

25. Other people's biggest misconception
    about me is _____ .

26. If you could go back in time and meet
    each other in kindergarten, would you
    know each other?
    What were you like then—
    shy, bossy, bratty?

27. *"There is no love sincerer
    than the love of food."*
    —*George Bernard Shaw*

Do you eat to live or live to eat?

28. What was the first car you ever owned?
    Did you buy it yourself?
    What was the best car you ever owned?

29. Go to a new restaurant together every two weeks.
Take turns choosing, and make your choice a surprise.

30. Do you like scary movies? What is the scariest film you've ever seen?

31. What do you think is your worst habit?
    What do others think your
    worst habit is?

32. Read each other's favorite book;
    discuss them, perhaps over brunch,
    at a picnic, or on a long walk.

33. What is the worst date
    you've ever been on?

34. Who is the craziest (creepy crazy) person you've ever met?
Who is the craziest (good crazy) person you've ever met?

35. Have you ever gone horseback riding, aside from pony rides at a fair?

36. *"It is so difficult for a sick man not to be a scoundrel."* —*Samuel Johnson*

What are you like when you are sick with a cold or the flu? Cranky? Whiny? Want to be left alone? Like company? Happy to be waited on?

37. How old were you when you learned to swim? Were you afraid of the water or was it impossible to keep you out of it?

38. How many cousins do you have? Who is your favorite?

39. What is your earliest memory? Does it involve sight, smell, sound, touch, or all of the above?

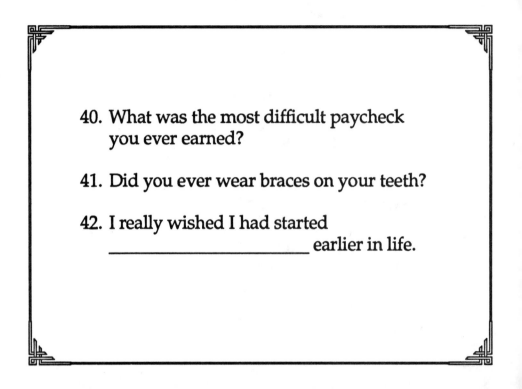

40. What was the most difficult paycheck you ever earned?

41. Did you ever wear braces on your teeth?

42. I really wished I had started _____ earlier in life.

43. *"The reports of my death are greatly exaggerated."* —Mark Twain

What's the closest you've come to dying? Did the experience change your way of living?

44. What was your best subject in school? Do you use that in your job today? Would you like to?

45. Do you believe in God?
    Do you consider yourself religious,
    and/or spiritually minded?

46. What foods upset your stomach?

47. If you could change sexes for one day,
    what do you imagine would intrigue you
    most about it?

48. Describe your mother in one word.

49. Describe your father in one word.

50. From a culinary standpoint,
    what is your specialty?

51. *"The profession of book writing makes horse racing seem like a solid, stable business."* —John Steinbeck

Have you ever thought about writing a book?

52. The last time you attended a costume party, how did you dress?

53. Which holiday do you like best?
    What do you like most about it?

54. Have you ever stayed overnight
    in a hospital?

55. If you knew you would die within one
    year, what would you do differently?

56. What's your favorite love song?
    What lyrics in the song do you like best?

57. *"Do you come here often?"*
"Only in the mating season."
                                    —*Spike Milligan*

What is the worst pick-up line
you ever heard?
What is the best?

58. Who taught you how to drive?
    How would you describe your driving?

59. What's your favorite comic strip?

60. Have you ever soaked in a natural
    hot spring?

61. What is your favorite thing to do that
    doesn't cost any money?

62. Describe how you learned to ride a bicycle.

63. What was your favorite TV show as a child? Five years ago? Today?

64. Go window shopping together and pick out your dream gifts.

65. If you were to be reincarnated as an animal, which would you choose?

66. Go through family photo albums together.

67. Take a class and learn something that you must do with another, such as ballroom dancing, massage, cooking for two, etc.

68. Which side of the bed do you like to sleep on?

69. What do you normally eat
    when you're alone?

70. As a child, did you ever climb into bed
    with your parents?

71. What parts of your life
    do you feel you control?
    How much of your life
    is controlled by forces beyond you?

72. Looking back on how you were raised, what do you and don't you want to repeat with your own children?

73. *"Man is the only animal that blushes. Or needs to."* —Mark Twain

    What was the most embarrassing situation you found yourself in?

74. Which of your high school teachers
    did you like the most? The least?

75. What would you like to do with
    each other that you have never done?

76. What was the toughest course
    you ever had in school?
    How did you get through it?

77. What is the lengthiest telephone conversation you've ever had? Do you like to talk on the phone?

78. When you met each other—
    What did you first notice?
    What did you like best?
    What did you want to know more about?
    Which part of their body intrigued you?
    What reservations did you have?

79. *"All things most people want to know*
are usually none of their business."
—*George Bernard Shaw*

Are you nosy by nature? Are you more
nosy about some things than others?

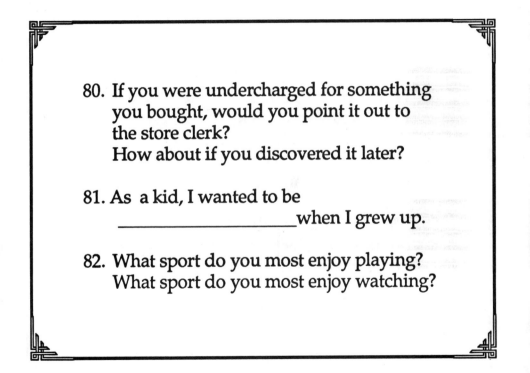

80. If you were undercharged for something you bought, would you point it out to the store clerk?
How about if you discovered it later?

81. As a kid, I wanted to be _____ when I grew up.

82. What sport do you most enjoy playing?
What sport do you most enjoy watching?

83. Have you ever bought a lottery ticket?
    Do you have any lucky numbers?

84. What is the most difficult decision
    you've ever had to make?

85. What was the one thing you were scared
    out of your wits to do but in retrospect
    are glad you did?

86. *"He pasted picture postcards around goldfish bowls to make the goldfish think they were going places."*
　　　　　　　　—*Fred Allen*

Where would you like to go
that you have never been?

87. When was the last time, if ever, you were really drunk?
Was it funny, horrible or both?

88. If time were no object, would train, plane, bus, car, boat or bicycle be your transportation of choice?

89. What is the one thing in life you haven't done that you regret not doing?

90. What place have you visited that you would most like to see again? Least?

91. If you could be an Olympic athlete in any sport, which would you choose?

92. *"No act of kindness, however small, is ever wasted."* —Æsop's Fables

Who is the kindest person you've ever known?

93. Do you eat anchovies?

94. *"It wasn't the wine,"* murmured
    Mr. Snodgrass in a broken voice,
    "It was the salmon."

    —Charles Dickens,
    The Pickwick Papers

Have you ever been sick in public?

95. If you had the choice of hiking to the top of a mountain or taking a cable car to the summit, which would you enjoy more?

96. Would you climb the steps to the top of the 555-foot Washington Monument?

97. To which fairy tale or children's book character do you most relate?

98. The best book I read in the past year was

_____ .

99. *"The sooner every party breaks up
   the better."*   —Jane Austen, Emma

Are you a party person?
What is the best party
you ever attended?

100. What was your proudest moment
as a child? As an adult?
What did you do to make your parents
proudest of you?

101. Have any of your friends died?

102. What book has had the most effect on
you?

103. *"The penalty for laughing in a courtroom is six months in jail; if it were not for this penalty, the jury would never hear the evidence."* —H.L. Mencken

Have you ever been unable to stop laughing, especially at an inappropriate time?

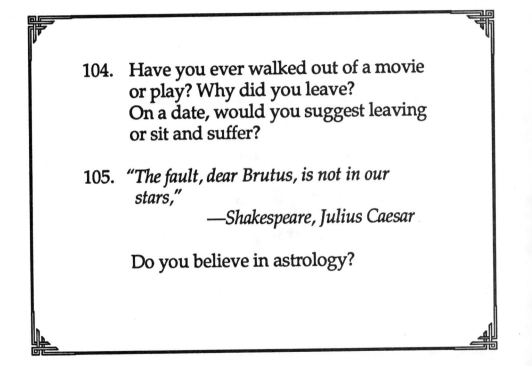

104. Have you ever walked out of a movie
     or play? Why did you leave?
     On a date, would you suggest leaving
     or sit and suffer?

105. *"The fault, dear Brutus, is not in our
     stars,"*
                              —Shakespeare, Julius Caesar

     Do you believe in astrology?

106. What were your grandparents like?

107. Do you ever skip ahead to read
the last page of a book?
Do you read one book at a time or
have several going at once?

108. Do you prefer to get your news from
TV, radio or newspapers?

109. Would you perjure yourself to protect someone you love?

110. If I start to feel a little sad, I _____ to cheer myself up.

111. What person were you the most nervous about meeting?

112. What is the all-time favorite piece of clothing you have ever owned?

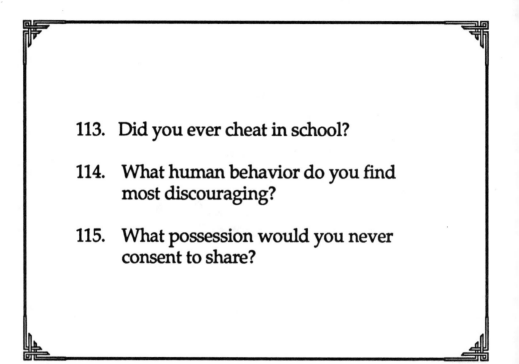

113. Did you ever cheat in school?

114. What human behavior do you find most discouraging?

115. What possession would you never consent to share?

116. *"I like long walks, especially when
they are taken by people who annoy me."*
—*Fred Allen*

When did you last go for a long walk?

117. If you could remain one age for your
entire life, which would you choose?

118. *"I suppose I overdo it, but when I'm mad at a man I want to climb right up his chest."* —*Theodore Roosevelt*

How do your express your anger?

119. When was the last time you cried?

120. _____ was the most depressing, saddest day of my life.

121. If you had to spend a year in jail,
     who would you want as a cellmate?

122. Who is the cruelest person
     you have ever known?

123. What are you working toward in your
     life? Do you have dreams of what
     you'd like to be or do?

124. *"They praise these but they read those."*
       —Martial, 1st century A.D.

   What was the last really trashy book
   you read?

125. Are you afraid of heights? Snakes? The
     dark? Spiders? Bad dreams? Flying?

126. Which song can bring tears
     to your eyes?
     Which can make you instantly happy?

127. Have you ever slept outdoors?

128. If you could choose any make, model and color of car, what would it be?

129. What foreign countries have you visited?
Which was the biggest surprise?
Where did you have the most fun?

130. How would you most like to be "spoiled"?

131. *"I know only two tunes; one of them is
'Yankee Doodle,' and the other isn't."*
                                    —*Ulysses S. Grant*

Do you sing when you're alone?

132. Which quality do you most admire in
people of the opposite sex?
Of your sex?

133. Which three qualities do you require
in a friendship?

134. If you had the choice of being
very good looking or very smart,
which would you choose?
For yourself?
For your partner?
For your child?

135. Have you ever won anything?
A competition requiring skill?
A game of chance?

136. Architecturally, what kind of house would you prefer to live in?

137. How would you break off a relationship of no further interest to you?

138. *"I wouldn't want to belong to a club that would accept me as a member."*
　　　　　　　　　　—*Groucho Marx*

What clubs or organizations do you belong to?
Which have you belonged to?

139. If you had to spend three months alone on an island, what possessions, besides essentials for survival, would you take?

140. Have you ever given testimony in court? Have you ever been on a jury?

141. What would you like to be doing five years from now? Is that goal realistic or wishful? Is your life now as you expected it would be five years ago?

142. If you were given $10,000 cash
that no one else knew about,
(including Uncle Sam)
what would you do with it?

143. Would you shave your head for $100?
How about $1,000?
What about $10,000?

144. When was the last time you
were in a library?

145. Have you ever broken one date to go on another date with someone else?

146. Who is your best friend of the opposite sex?

147. Do you know CPR?

148. Whose voice do you find particularly soothing? Irritating?

149. *"There are few wild beasts more to be dreaded than a talking man having nothing to say."* —Jonathan Swift

With whom do you most dread being cornered in a conversation?

150. When making a phone call to someone you don't know, would you rather speak to an answering machine or a human being?

151. If you were running late for an
     appointment and a foreign visitor
     tried to ask directions,
     would you stop to help him or her?

152. *"I never sleep comfortably except
     when I am at sermon or praying."*
     —*Rabelais*

     Have you ever fallen asleep at an
     inappropriate time?

153. What social event did you go to kicking and screaming but were later glad you attended?

154. If you're home alone do you shut the door when you use the bathroom?

155. If you were casting a film about your life, who would play the main characters?

156. Whenever I'm beginning to feel bored,
     I _____ .

157. Have you ever seriously
     wished someone dead?

158. If you had to choose, would you rather
     have three very good friends or
     unlimited acquaintances?

159. *"Brevity is the soul of lingerie."*
                                              —Dorothy Parker

(If you are a woman) Do you like to wear sexy lingerie? What is your favorite article of underwear?
(If you are a man) Do you find lingerie sexy on a woman?

160. Do you ever cry when you're happy?

161. Write an epitaph for your own tombstone.

162. How long do you normally sleep each night? Do you need that much every night or can you function on less?

163. Have you ever been in a fist fight?

164. *"Coffee should be black as hell,*
strong as death, and sweet as love."
—*Turkish proverb*

How do you take your coffee?
Have you always taken it that way?

165. What was your worst physical injury?
Do you think it changed your way of
looking at things?

166. What did you think of the last video you rented?

167. *"I am dying with the help of too many physicians."* —Alexander the Great

Did you ever feel so sick that you just wished you could die?

168. If you could change one of your physical characteristics, what would it be?

169. If you could change one attribute of your personality, which would it be?

170. My favorite television commercial of all time is _____.

171. Where would you like to have a vacation home? Why?

172. Have you ever been with someone
as he or she was dying?

173. *"Happiness: a good bank account, a
good cook and a good digestion."*
        —*Jean-Jacques Rousseau*

How do you define happiness?

174. What member of your family do you
feel closest to?
Why do you feel that way?

175. Would you rather spend two weeks crossing the Atlantic to Europe on a luxury cruise ship or fly first class and spend two weeks in the city of your choice?

176. Would you rather be famous but just comfortable financially, or extremely wealthy but anonymous? Why?

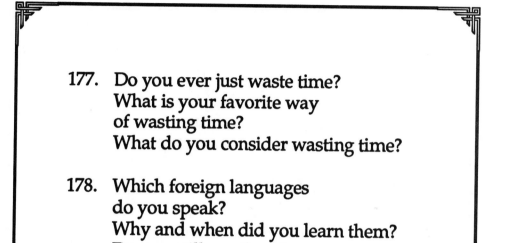

177. Do you ever just waste time?
What is your favorite way
of wasting time?
What do you consider wasting time?

178. Which foreign languages
do you speak?
Why and when did you learn them?
Do you still use them?

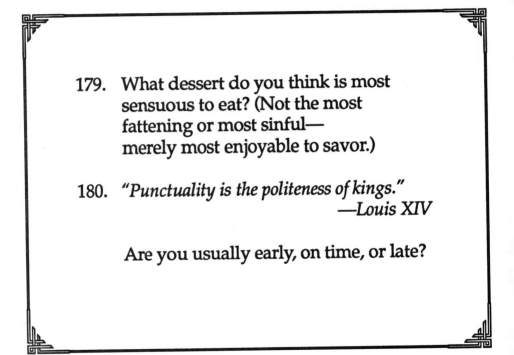

179. What dessert do you think is most sensuous to eat? (Not the most fattening or most sinful— merely most enjoyable to savor.)

180. *"Punctuality is the politeness of kings."*
        —*Louis XIV*

    Are you usually early, on time, or late?

181. If you wanted to flirt with someone how would you normally get his or her attention?
    Do you consider yourself a good flirt?
    Do you like flirting?

182. Have you been embarrassed by a date's behavior in public?

183. Probably my greatest fear in life is

    _____ .

184. When you get up in the middle of the night, what is your midnight drink? What is your midnight munchie?

185. How many states in the United States have you visited? Have you ever gone to a National Park or other natural wonder?

186. *"If you go long enough without a bath,*
     even the fleas will leave you alone."
                                        —*Ernie Pyle*

   What is the longest you've ever gone
   without bathing?

187. When you were growing up
    did your family usually have dinner
    together, or did you all eat whenever
    you had time?

188. If someone described you as finicky, what would he or she be talking about? Do you think you are finicky?

189. *"Over in Hollywood they almost made a great picture, but they caught it just in time."* —Wilson Mizner

What was the most boring movie you ever saw?

190. What kind of shopper are you?
Do you love to shop or do you do it
only out of necessity?
Do you search for the best prices,
or do you just walk into a store and
buy what you like?

191. Have you ever bought something you
didn't need, just because it was
a great bargain?

192. Have you ever vacationed alone?
     What did you like best and least
     about it?

193. What is the silliest thing you ever
     did on purpose in public?
     How about unintentionally?

194. Who is the most eccentric friend you
     have? What makes him or her
     so eccentric?

195. *"There are more tears shed over answered prayers than unanswered ones."* —St. Teresa of Avila

What childhood or high school dreams are you now glad never came true?

196. If your house were on fire,
     what is the one possession you'd grab
     before you ran out?

197. What is your home remedy for a cold?
     How well does it work?
     Where did you learn it?

198. What is your cure for the hiccups?
     What is the craziest cure you have
     ever heard of?

199. *"I have learned that success is to be measured not so much by the position one has achieved . . . but by the obstacles . . . overcome while trying to succeed."*
        —Booker T. Washington

How do you define success?

200. What household chore did you hate the most when you were young?
Are there any you enjoyed?

201. Did you ever want to trade lives
with someone else? Who and why?

202. What New Year's resolutions did you
make this year?
How long did you keep them?

203. Which movie did you see in the past
year that made you laugh most?

204. Have you ever made a fire
and cooked over it?
(Backyard barbecues don't count.)

205. Are you a good letter writer?
How many people do you owe letters?

206. Do you ever give advice when you
really don't know what you're
talking about?

207. Many people only will accept "the best." What do you know so well and enjoy so much that you never accept less than the best?

208. What are the three superstitions you heard most while you were growing up?
Do you still believe any of them?

209. *"I can live for two months on a good*
compliment." —*Mark Twain*

Do you accept compliments easily
or do they make you feel
uncomfortable?
What uplifting compliment have you
received lately?

210. Have you ever wanted to be an actor?
     What show would you like to be in?

211. Did you get an allowance when you
     were a kid? How much?
     Did you have to earn it?
     How did you spend it?

212. What sport do you most enjoy playing
     with a partner?

213. What ability do you wish you had that you don't have?

214. Overall, would you consider yourself a procrastinator? In which area of your life do you procrastinate most?

215. During what part of the day do you feel most creative?
Do you feel more creative when alone or with other people?

216. Do you have any special places you like to go to think things out?

217. If Santa Claus walked in the door right now, what would be the perfect gift he could bring?

218. If you were having a dinner party for six, of all the people in the world, dead or alive, whom would you invite?

219. *"Never tell people <u>how</u> to do a thing. Tell them <u>what</u> to do and they will surprise you with their ingenuity."*
—*George Patton*

What is the most elegant solution to a problem you ever came up with?

220. What is your favorite season?
What do you like most about it?

221. What is your favorite activity in
each season—
winter, spring, summer, fall?

222. Did anyone ever read you bedtime
stories? What was your favorite?

223. Would you rather be married to a famous person, or be famous yourself?

224. What is outlawed that you wish wasn't?

225. Have you ever driven all night to get to a destination?

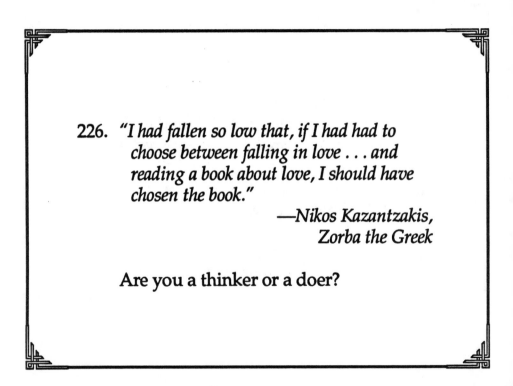

226. *"I had fallen so low that, if I had had to choose between falling in love . . . and reading a book about love, I should have chosen the book."*

—*Nikos Kazantzakis,*
Zorba the Greek

Are you a thinker or a doer?

227. Go to the zoo together and visit three animals that you both especially like. Observe them, and guess which of their characteristics appeal most to the other person.

228. Have you ever been to a circus in a tent?

229. Did you cram all night before any exams? All exams?

230. What is the last good deed you did?

231. If a genie rose out of a bottle and gave you three wishes, what would they be? (yes we know this question is overworked, but the answers are irresistibly revealing)

232. What do you enjoy doing, even consider fun, that most other people regard as hard work?

233. Have you ever wanted a tattoo?

234. Do you believe in fate?
Has anything ever happened to you
that made you believe in it or not?

235. Have you ever hated anyone?
Why? Do you still feel that way?

236. Do you have any talents or skills that
were once polished but have gotten
rusty for lack of practice?

237. *"Will you, won't you, will you, won't you,*
will you join the dance?"
—Lewis Carroll, *The Lobster Quadrille*
from Alice in Wonderland

Do you like to dance?
When and where was the last time you
got to really dance?
Do you know ballroom dancing with
the *right* steps—waltz, tango,
foxtrot or polka?

238. Have you ever performed (acting, playing music, singing, dancing, making speeches, etc.) in public? Did you enjoy it?

239. Do you prefer to work alone or with a group?

240. Do you more often do what you *want* to do or what you feel you *should* do?

241. When was the last time you stopped yourself from doing what you wanted just because it wouldn't look right?

242. What room in your house or apartment do you enjoy most? Why?

243. Do you find it an occasional relief to use bad language?

244. *"A man never knows what a fool he is*
until he hears himself imitated by one."
—*Herbert Beerbohm Tree*

Can you do a really good imitation of
anyone or anything?
Pretty good? Lousy?

245. Which friends from school do you still
     stay in touch with?
     Where do they live today and
     what do they do?
     When was the last time you spoke?

246. Do you go to class reunions?

247. With whom have you been friends longest? When was the last time you saw him or her?

248. Were you a good student in school? Do you wish you had studied more or goofed off more?

249. If you had to eat the same food for three days in a row, what would it be?

250. Which magazines do you read regularly, and which do you enjoy the most and spend the most time reading?

251. Some people write, others call on the phone, others spend hours looking for the perfect card.
How do you most often communicate your feelings to close friends when they are not near?

252. When you have something difficult to say or complicated to explain, which works better for getting your point across—writing or talking ?

253. How do you keep your life organized? Lists? Appointment book? Computer? All or none of the above?

254. *Just answer these questions, my dear;*
You really have nothing to fear:
You're not under oath,
And we'll answer them both—
Who knows, this may make it all clear!

Do you know any limericks?
Have you ever made any up?

255. Does your family have strong traditions that you still observe and plan to pass on to future family generations?

256. When was the last time you gave someone advice that turned out to be just the thing he or she should have done?

257. Do you think "free advice" is worth what anyone pays for it?

258. "My handwriting looks as if a swarm of
     ants, escaping from an ink bottle, had
     walked over a sheet of paper without
     wiping their legs."   —Sydney Smith

Write your names or a short sentence,
then analyze what your signature and
handwriting say about each of you.

259. When you go on vacation do you ever read books? If you do, what kinds of books do you read?

260. Do you make a budget and follow it? Do you balance your checkbook?

261. If you had an extra day every month that no one else had, what are the ways you would spend it?

262. Are you physically affectionate?
     What is your limit to being touched by
     platonic friends—touching on the arm,
     hugging, kissing on the cheek,
     kissing on closed lips?

263. How did you spend your last
     birthday? New Year's Eve? Vacation?

264. *"Life consists not in holding good cards*
but in playing those you do hold, well."
—Josh Billings

Do you consider yourself a gambler in
life? What was the last thing you
considered a gamble?
Did you win or lose?

265. *"Mankind is divisible into two great classes: hosts and guests."*

—*Max Beerbohm*

Which role do you enjoy more?

266. When you think you are being conservative and safe, do others think you are taking wild chances?

267. Do you believe in an afterlife?

268. Do you consider yourself
     smoothly diplomatic
     or brutally honest?

269. *"Save me, oh save me, from the
     Candid Friend."*   —*Canning*

     When do you feel that honesty
     is *not* the best policy?

270. Have you ever participated in a dangerous sport such as skydiving, hang gliding, scuba diving, running the bulls, or bungee jumping?

271. If your answer to the question above is yes, what do you enjoy most about these activities? If your answer is no, why not? Are you afraid to try, or have you just not had the chance?

272. Do you add up the bill at a restaurant or just pay without checking?

273. *"I never found the companion that was so companionable as solitude."*
   —*Thoreau*

   Do you like being alone, or do you need someone around most of the time? What do you like about being alone?

274. Would you rather live safely, watch what you eat, and exercise to live longer, or live an exciting, eventful life and enjoy all the bad things but live a short time?

275. *"Saving enriches and spending impoverishes."* —Samuel Johnson

Which do you enjoy more — spending or saving?

276. What is your favorite color?

277. Describe your idea of a perfect romantic evening, start to finish.

278. What is the best way anyone could compliment you about your work?

279. Describe your most memorable family vacation.

280. *"If it doesn't out and out kill you, it will
make you stronger."*
—*Native American proverb*

Share past difficulties that have made
you a better person, or from which you
have learned important lessons.

281. What do you feel you do in excess?

282. Are you good at "faking it" when you're not exactly sure what to do? Describe the last time you faked it and got away with it.

283. *"Let's fight till six and then have dinner," said Tweedledum.*
    —*Lewis Carroll, Through the Looking-Glass*

    Are you argumentative or do you let disagreements ride to keep peace at any price?

284. Which person do you respect the most in the world?

285. *"Why walk five miles to fish when you can be just as unsuccessful closer to home?"*
— Mark Twain

Have you ever caught a fish?
Do you like to go fishing?
What kind of fishing is your favorite?

286. *"Whenever I feel like exercise, I lie down until the feeling passes."*

—Robert Hutchins

Have you ever belonged to a health club? Did you use it mainly for exercise or to meet people?

287. What do you think is your most attractive physical feature?

288. Do you think you're persistent or more of a quitter? What actions of yours demonstrate this?

289. As a child, were you closer to your mother or your father? Which one are you closer to now?

290. What new activity or interest would you like to make space for in your life?

291. Would you go through an 8-item checkout line with ten items? What would you do if you had six items and the person in front of you had 15 or 20?

292. Describe to each other the best and worst aspects of your jobs.

293. What kind of photographer are you? How do you organize your photographs and slides?

294. *"Greater love hath no man than this,
that a man lay down his life for his
friends."* —*John 15:13*

Under what circumstances could you
see yourself doing this?

295. What adult toy are you most fussy
about? Your car, stereo, video
collection and system, gourmet
kitchen, boat, airplane, skis?

296. *"The Moving Finger writes;*
and having writ,
Moves on: nor all thy Piety nor Wit
Shall lure it back to cancel half a Line,
Nor all thy Tears wash out a Word of it."
—*The Rubáiyát of Omar Khayyám*

If you could go back, what event or
thing would you change in your life ?

297. What do you like to do on a rainy
     Saturday (or other day off?)
     Note: If you live in Seattle, substitute
     "sunny" for "rainy."

298. What was the last thing you watched
     someone do that impressed
     the hell out of you?

299. Do you clip discount coupons?
     Do you *use* them? Or do they pile up
     and eventually expire?

300. *"Please return this book; I find that though many of my friends are poor arithmeticians, they are nearly all good bookkeepers."* —Sir Walter Scott

Do you owe books to any friends?
Do any friends owe you books?

301. What kind of tipper are you?
Why do you tip that way?

302. If you were in a non-smoking section and someone lit up, would you ask him or her to stop? Ask a waitress or usher to do it? Ask to move? Do nothing?

303. What ethnic food do you like best—Thai, Chinese, Mexican, Indian, Ethiopian, French?

304. Which birthday party do you remember enjoying the most?

305. Are you an early bird or a night owl?

306. Describe the aromas that evoke vivid memories for you.

307. *"Men will confess to treason, murder, arson, false teeth, or a wig. But how many will own up to a lack of humor!"*
    —*Frank Moore Colby*

   What kind of sense of humor do you feel you have—
   sarcastic, dry, witty, jovial?

308. What kind of a pet did you have as a
kid? If you didn't have a pet, why not?
Do you have a pet now?
What kind would you like to have?

309. *"Your children are not your children.
They are the sons and daughters of
life's longing for itself."* —Khalil Gibran

Do you like to be around children?
What ages do you think are the cutest?
The most difficult?

310. _____ would be the worst way to die.

311. Do you think that you look better wearing clothes or naked?

312. Do you own a personal computer? What do you use it for in your everyday life?

313. If you could think up a new invention
     to use around the house,
     what would it do?

314. *"America is the country where you
     buy a lifetime supply of aspirin for one
     dollar and use it up in two weeks."*
     —*Fred Allen*

     Do you get headaches?
     How frequently?

315. Do you like gardening?
     Did you ever grow anything in your
     garden that you actually ate?

316. What kinds of handyman tasks
     can you do best?
     If you have the time, do you prefer to
     fix things yourself?

317. Do you change the oil in your car,
     or do you have someone else do it?

318. What three things stress you out most on a daily basis?

319. *"Beware of all enterprises which require new clothes."* —*Thoreau*

When is the last time you went on a clothes shopping spree?

320. What music do you like to listen to while making love?

321. What was the last live performance you saw? Was it a musical, a play, a concert, the church choir, your daughter's ballet recital?

322. Which stations is your car radio tuned to? What kind of radio program do you enjoy most on the highway? In bumper-to-bumper traffic?

323. How many newspapers do you read a week? Which ones? Do you have a favorite column? Which papers do you prefer for different types of news?

324. What is your favorite piece of artwork? Is it a painting, print, sculpture, ancient artifact? Modern, medieval, ethnographic, Renaissance?

325. What way of life in what climate would you consider a dream existence?

326. Do you believe in these proverbial sayings? Describe how you learned they were true or untrue.

A stitch in time saves nine.
Easier said than done.
A bird in the hand is worth two in the bush.
Don't count your chickens before they hatch.
Don't cry over spilt milk.
We'll cross that bridge when we come to it.

327. What do you think is your most unusual talent (like standing on your head, wiggling your ears, playing the spoons, juggling)?

328. What makes you feel guilty?

329. What qualities do you now recognize in someone you used to know that went unappreciated at the time?

330. If you could live in the past,
what era would you pick—
the Roman Empire, classical Greece,
Victorian England, King Arthur's
court, the hippie days of the 60s,
the Wild West, colonial America,
the Roaring 20s, the Stone Age?

331. What do you normally do for lunch at
work? Go out to a restaurant, grab a
sandwich at a deli, wolf down fast
food, or brown-bag it at your desk?

332. Are you an expert at anything?
(Gourmet food, movies, wines, cigars,
sex, Jeopardy, sports?)

333. On Sunday mornings I normally

_____ .

334. Do you enjoy bargaining for things
(at a flea market, for example)?
Have you ever pulled off a real coup
buying or selling anything?

335. *"We only confess our little faults to persuade people that we have no large ones."* —*La Rochefoucauld*

Confess to three tiny faults and one giant one.

336. What is your idea of a long trip? What's the longest trip you ever went on? (Distance? Time?)

337. If you still are in contact with your first love but are now involved with another, would you feel uncomfortable introducing your first love to your current partner?

338. Have you ever gone to a striptease show? (Women: this includes Chippendales and strip-a-grams.)

339. *"Congress is in session and
no man is safe."* —Mark Twain

How important is voting in national
and local elections to you?

340. If your election were guaranteed,
would you ever run for public office?
If so, which one? If not, why not?

341. What kinds of jobs did you have as a kid—newspaper route, baby sitting, washing dishes, mowing lawns?

342. Can you play any musical instruments? Which ones? Decently? What would you like to play?

343. Which shows or events have you wanted to attend so much that you bought tickets from scalpers? Was it worth it?

344. *"Three may keep a secret if two of them are dead."* —*Benjamin Franklin*

Are you good at keeping secrets?
Do you feel uncomfortable when asked to keep a secret?

345. If you own a microwave oven, do you actually use it to cook, or only to warm food and coffee or make popcorn?

346. *"I don't care who you are, what your other car is, or what you'd rather be doing."*   —*Bumper sticker*

Do you feel a need to share your opinions with others? Do you sometimes wish others wouldn't share so many of theirs with you?

347. What movie have you recently seen that made you cry?
Were they tears of joy or sadness?

348. *"You can observe a lot by watching."*
                                    —*Yogi Berra*

   What are your powers of observation?
   Sit with your backs to one another and
   jot down how you would physically
   describe the other person.

349. What do you normally
   daydream about?

350. What are you most obsessive about? Why? Are your records and CD's organized alphabetically and by type of music? Are your clothes organized in the closet by type and color, etc.?

351. Have you ever gone to a party or other function very overdressed or underdressed for the occasion? If you had to stand out at a party, would you rather be too fancy or too casual?

352. What were your high school activities? Were you on the newspaper or yearbook staff, a majorette, on the debating team, or an athlete?

353. What subject or story would you like to make a movie about?

354. What is your favorite museum? What do you like most about it?

355. *"The dream is the theater where the dreamer is at once scene, actor, prompter, stage manager, author, audience, and critic."* —Carl Jung

Do you remember your dreams? Do you have any that recur?

356. What food or beverage did you enjoy being served on a childhood visit to a grandparent's or other relative's home?

357. What kind of store do you like poking around in most?
A toy store, bookstore, kitchen gadget store, auto parts store, hardware store, sporting goods store, etc.?

358. By the year 2000, I hope _____ will be a reality.

359. Is there anything you wish you had told someone, but didn't? Is it too late?

360. Describe your last family reunion. How large is your family? How many of your family members made it to the reunion? What kinds of activities did you have together?

361. What is your favorite way to unwind, relax and pamper yourself after a tough day?

362. What's the most exotic place you've ever gone swimming?

363. What destination would be most romantic for you? Let these images kindle your imagination:

Venice with its gondolas,
Paris with the Latin Quarter,
London's cozy pubs,
A sunset in the South Pacific,
Floating through the deep jungle,
The Taj Mahal by full moon,
A horse-drawn sleigh ride in New England.

362. *"An optimist is a fellow who believes a housefly is looking for a way to get out."*
   —*George Jean Nathan*

   Do you consider yourself an optimist or a pessimist?

363. Do you consider yourself an idealist or a realist? A conformist or nonconformist? Have you changed during your life?

365. *"Animals are such agreeable friends;*
they ask no questions,
they pass no criticisms."

—*George Eliot*

What is the most interesting question
anyone ever asked you?

We hope you've enjoyed this book.
We'd love to see your answer to the last question as well any
other questions you feel we should include in future editions.
Charlie and Jeanne, World Leisure Corporation
PO Box 160, Hampstead, NH 03841